CIARA LEWIS

The ANCHOR HOLDS

BOOK OF POETRY

Dedication

I dedicate this book in memory of my grandmother and my uncle, may they rest in peace.

My grandmother and uncle were two of my biggest fans of my poetry. They would always tell me that I needed to make it into a book and submit it somewhere. I really didn't know much about publishing at the time and knew it wasn't something to just rush into. I knew when the time was right, I would get it done. My uncle passed in March of 2020 and my grandmother passed in May of 2020. So, it is a true honor to be able to have this book published exactly 5 years and 5 days after my grandmother's passing to celebrate their anniversaries. I know they would love this book and would be super proud of my accomplishment in getting it published.

RIP granny and uncle K until we meet again. With Love always!

Introduction

The Anchor Holds draws inspiration from a variety of real-life events and experiences I've encountered throughout my life. Much of the material emerged spontaneously, often receiving direct messages from The Creator himself. I have always written from the depths of my heart, reflecting my emotions in the process. My writing journey began in middle school, where I crafted short stories before shifting my focus to poetry. I appreciate the power of poetry, as it conveys profound messages in a concise format. My passion for this art form led me to participate in several poetry contests, and I was honored to win my first contest with a poem I dedicated to my grandmother, titled "Watching Over ME." I have compiled my poems into a collection aimed at inspiring and uplifting others during challenging times. The themes of my work span a wide array of genres, including Birthdays, Friendships and Relationships, Daughters, Mothers, Fathers, Valentine's Day, Religion and Spirituality, Babyhood and Childhood, Grief, Domestic Violence, and more.

Contact Me:

Website: http://fierceandfearlessentrepreneur.com
Email: fiercefearlessentrepreneur2025@gmail.com
Phone: 606-767-5025

Table of Contents

Prelude

Why is it that we want so badly for certain things, but then sometimes once we get them, we don't pay them any attention, or let them go to waste? But why is that when we wanted it so badly in the beginning? But then, once it's gone or not working anymore, then we wish we had it back or paid more attention to it when we first had it. Like that new toy for Christmas that we asked for all year, we finally get it and play with it twice, only to leave it in the closet or basement for the rest of the year.

I said that to say this: GOD wants us to want Him and love Him and not just for a second and then put Him to the side. He wants us to want and need Him all the time and every second of our day. Material things will never fulfill your needs the way GOD can spiritually, mentally, and emotionally. GOD needs and deserves our attention all the time. We should feel the same way about GOD the way we do when we get that new phone, new toy, new shoes, new car, or whatever it may be. But we should keep our attention on Him and always keep Him by our side, no matter what is going on in life. GOD doesn't like borrowed time.

Birthdays

Happy Sweet Birthday To A Mom Like You

Happy sweet birthday to a mom like you.
You're a daughter's dream come true
My life would be empty without you.
You showed me motherhood and how to love too
I thank GOD every day for a wonderful woman like you.

You're strong at heart and beautiful and smart.
You're the reason I had a journey in life to start.
We may grow old and watch time go by,
But no matter what, we will never fall apart.
For you have always held the key to my heart.

Happy Birthday, Mom, and may GOD BLESS you.
I thank GOD for another year with you, too.
You have held my hand all the way through, and now it's
time
For me to help you along the way, too.
So, take my hand as we travel, we have so many stories
and roads to unravel.
It will be fun, I promise you this, it will be an adventure you
don't want to miss.

Happy Birthday, Mom

6/5/18

Eleven Years Ago

Eleven years ago, you warmed my deep soul.
When I felt your little feet kick, I couldn't wait for you to grow.
Now that time has passed, and you have grown too fast, I often wonder where did the time go?
I wish I could rewind the clock and make time go slow.
I just love to sit and watch you, because you have such a beautiful glow.
You will do just fine in life and will go with the flow.
There are a lot of things you still don't know.
But in due time, GOD will let them show.
So, hold on tight and never let Him go, for He is always with you even when it doesn't seem so.
He will guide you all the way, and you will have no reason to ever be afraid.

Happy Birthday, baby girl!! I love you more than you will know.

57th Birthday

You're turning fifty-seven, what a great gift from heaven. Sometimes still wondering what life is bringing. Thank GOD up above because He's with you even when it's raining. Even when things don't go the way you were thinking, no need to worry, because you're still precious in GOD's ranking. It's been a long road getting to fifty-seven. But you always know you're still on the road to heaven. Happy Birthday to you, and may it be the best one too.

To:
Aunt Lee (3-16-16)

Happy Birthday, My Friend

Happy Birthday, my friend,
Happy Birthday to you
It's sure been a blessing spending all these years with you.
You have always been there for me, to help me see things through.
My life would be empty if I didn't have you. Sometimes, I often wonder
what I would do if I didn't have someone as special as you? Times have
changed, but so have we, no need to worry for friends we will always be.
We have had our ups and downs, but no matter what, we will always be around. Friends are great, but Best Friends are better because no
matter what, they will always stick together. I love you, sis, with all
my heart and pray our friendship never grows apart.

67th Birthday

You're turning sixty-seven, apparently. You raised your kids successfully, and grandchildren too, especially. You've done so well independently; life is short, but some people can't see what a true blessing it is to turn sixty-seven. I'm glad we can spend this birthday with you, on this day that was meant just for you, especially.

To:
Granny (3/16/1

April 2nd Is The Day

April 2nd is the day. The day the LORD has made. He made this day especially for you, as he promised to see you through. He knows the road you've traveled and the stories you've unraveled. You still have a long journey to go, but he'll hold your hand and help you get through it nice and slow. This special day was made for you, we hope you enjoy it and have a good one too. We thank GOD for this day he made specifically for you.

Friendships/ Relationships

Close In Heart

Far away, but close in heart.
Together, we chose this journey to start.
Where it leads or where we will go, only time will tell that.
This journey will show.
We will fall and we will grow, but our love will conquer and
let our true souls show.
It will reveal the deep secrets that only you and I will know.
The journey may be long and may be rough, but only love
like ours can handle the tough.
Keep holding on and fighting strong.
I'll meet you at the end, soldier, for it will not be long.

Your Footprints
Always Follow Us

Your footprints always follow us everywhere we go.
Every move we make, somehow you always know.
Your eyes are always watching us as we continue to grow.
You're always keeping up with us even as you grow old.
Your heart has never given up on us nor ever grown cold.
You've always been good to us and been the food for our
soul.
We always know you're with us, as we feel your love flow.
We know where to follow you, because you have such a
glow.
We each love you more than you know, and it's not just
because we tell you so.

Happy Birthday Nana  !!!

We love you 🤍🤍🤍

A Letter To A Best Friend

I don't know how to write a letter to a best friend,
To try and tell her it feels like our friendship has come to
an
end.
We stretched it far and even watched it bend. But
sometimes
Things break and have to be amended.
We were always like glue, too strong to break.
Somehow, our bond broke, and we need to bring it back
in.
Best friends are hard to find, and they fight until the end.
Let's not let the band break, let's bring it back in. For if we
Stretch too far, it will surely break from end to end.
Let's think back to where our friendship began and agree
to
Never let the rubber band stretch too far again.

To: My Best Friend (5/18/18)

Broken Heart

You broke my heart from the start,
Yet here we still are.
I want to go, I want to leave,
But for some reason, you will not let me be.
After all these years and long drawn-out tears,
I finally realized you're not the man for me.
I loved you dearly, but quite frankly
I'm tired of doing this yearly.
I love you, I do, with all my heart.
But I can't let this be the way I completely fall apart.

(4/18/18)

Disappearance

One minute, you're here and then you disappear.
You're almost like a ghost walking in thin air.
You're silent when I need you, but show when you want to.
That's made it very hard for me to believe in you.
You would tell me what I wanted to hear,
But funny how I would turn around and you would always
disappear.
When you felt like you needed us, you would reappear to
me.
But only for a second to make me believe you really
wanted it
to be.
It's too bad you can't see how much you have damaged
me,
I was good to you, but you were the only one who couldn't
see.
Now it's time to finally let each other be.

(4-26-18)

Friendships Don't Last

Life is short, friends are, too.
I'm not really sure what happened to me and you.
Sometimes, I wonder if you see it, too?
How much time has been lost between me and you?
I feel like we are almost saying our friendship is through.
People change, and friendships do, too, but I never
thought this
would happen with me and you.
We were so close, but now so far.
I've started to wonder who we really are.
I miss us hanging out together, but unfortunately, not all
Friendships last forever.

To: My Best Friend (5-2-18)

My Love For You

I love you with all my heart, even though we are
a little ways apart, but you're still my daddy deep
within my heart. I love you so much and I just want you
to know, that no matter what, my love will never get old.
You're so special to me, and I want you to see that no one
else could be that perfect daddy GOD created just for me.
I may get old and continue to grow, but you should know
my love for you will always continue to flow.

(2-15-16)

The Disappearing Act

There is only one act, that's the best part of the show.
It's the disappearing act, that everyone knows.
You do it quite well, but it's like show and don't tell.
But you keep it on the low.
You don't want people to know it's you they can't count on to
be there now.
It's the best act of the show, but when you don't come
back, it's
really kind of low.
It leaves people wondering where did you really go?
A true magician always comes back to finish off his show.
Are you coming back, or is it just a slacking act?
Don't worry, I can tell, because I know for a fact.
At the end of the show, and you're still not here,
Don't worry, it's nothing, you always disappear.
Congrats on your act, and good luck with that, because
the
person you loved is never coming back.

(4-26-18)

For The Days I Longed

For the days I longed to be with you.
I've always seen you and not just straight through.
I saw the good man you have in you.
I knew one day I would fall in love with you.
I just never knew it would be so soon.
You're my sun and my moon.
Your love fills me up like a hot air balloon.

The Day You Let Go

You held my hand and then you let go.
You kissed my lips but then walked away slowly.
You held me tight, but then disappeared slowly.
I asked you once, would you stay or would you go?
You left me behind and never said what you would do.
That's not what I expected of you.
I thought this was something you wanted, too.
You looked at me, and I looked at you, and this is what we
both once said we wanted to do.
You let go and expected me to, but there will never be a
day I will go without thinking of you.

When I Finally Give Up

When I finally give up,
Then you know I'm really through.
I'm finally done playing the games with you.
I've waited too long for five years through.
And I still have seen no good change in you.
I waited too long for you to come on,
But instead, you thought that no matter what, she will still tag along.
You probably haven't realized I really am gone,
That's so sad that it took this long.
I try so hard to really not miss you,
But it's so hard knowing all we went through.
But it's time to go, and I just pray you really know.
Because now all I can say is I told you so.

You Let Your Love Hide Away

You let your love hide away because you're afraid of what
others will say.
How do you do it, and hide the pain away?
Do you not think I'll disappear someday?
It's hard to let go every day, because I know you still care in
some special way.

It's been about you and never me.
How could you be so blind and never see?
You said you loved me, but how could that be?
You spent more time trying to flee.
Your love for me was never free.
I still pay the price, and it will never be.
After all these years, you tried to contain me
And ignored my love that you chose not to see.

Heart Be Still

Heart, be still, help find if this love is real.
This journey has been long, but quite a thrill.
Time has passed, but this love I can still feel.
Help my heart to finally heal and show me this is the real
deal.
If this is real, please let the rest of time stand still.

My Love For You Is Like Pure Gold

My love for you is like pure gold.
It's a special recipe that only you will ever know.
My love for you will never grow old, it's like a fountain that will continue to flow.
I hope you cherish it wherever you go, for I am always with you, I promise you so.
I will never ever let you go, I will hold on to you until GOD gives the final say so.
Until then, I will cherish you to the end and walk with you all the way through.
I want to spend every second with you, and spend the rest of my life with you, too.
I hope you cherish me as much as I cherish you.

Something About That Kiss That Day

There was something about that kiss that day.
Something that made me feel, that you would always stay.
I knew you would never truly shy away.
I knew even if you would stray, you somehow would
always come back my way.
I knew you cared about me in your own way,
I hoped you would come back for me someday.
That someday is now finally today, and I can't tell you how
happy I am you came back to stay.

Daughter's Poems

"

A daughter may
outgrow your lap, but
she will never outgrow
your heart

Don't Let Go

Hold my hand, don't let go.
Let me show you the world, so you will know.
It's good, it's bad, and some parts that will make you really sad. But if you listen now, it'll save you later and hold on to the knowledge that others wish they had. There are lies that people tell and a lot of truth to unveil. But don't worry, you have GOD's Grace and Mercy to keep you from the bad parts that will one day be unveiled.

Down The Aisle

She walked down the aisle with a beautiful white smile.
She was ready to take his hand and travel the long mile.
She knew it was a journey they wanted to travel, but she
had so much excitement to see what their journey would
unravel. She knew there would be ups and downs, and
even sometimes there would be some frowns. But at the
end of the day, she knew she had married one of the best
men GOD ever made. The journey would be long, but she
knew they were both strong, and she knew he really loved
her all along. As they
look at each other and say "I do," they pray every night that
GOD will see them through.

Sweet Girl, I Love You

Sweet girl, I love you more than you know,
There are not enough ways for me to show.
My love for you will continue to grow.
You make my heartbeat and love overflow.
I will love you forever, but only slow.
One day I'll look up and say, Where did the time go?
I'll follow you wherever you may go.
I'm always with you, for you should always know.
I will keep loving you, even as you grow.
My eyes grow weak, as all the tears flow.
I'm always thinking of how to let it show.
Fifty-plus ways and still some to go.
You have the most beautiful, sweet, and caring soul.

My Sweet Girl

My sweet daughter, I love you so.
I love to watch you learn and grow.
I'll never be ready to let you go.
I'll always be here by your side, so you'll know.
Your love for me melts my soul.
I wish I had all the ways to show just how much my love
for
you will always overflow.
When you go far, just close your eyes and hear my voice
You'll know in there and haven't let go.
I love you so and I want you to know, you'll always be my
baby
even when you get old.

From Day One I've Been Watching You

From day one, I've been watching you.
Watching you grow and seeing how you glow.
My love for you continues to grow.
You're my baby girl, and I just want you to know,
That I will always be by your side as you continue to grow.
We may not always agree, but someday you will have to leave.
That's why our time is so very important to me.
But even when it's time to leave, our love will always forever be.

Growing Love

Growing more and more every day.
It's hard being the perfect mother when you run out of the
right things to say.
You're beautiful and smart and have always had my heart.
It's been a true blessing watching you grow from the start.
Keep believing and keep on achieving.
If you stick with me, never worry about me leaving.
I'll hold your hand when life gets tough,
But don't worry, it's not always rough.
I'll wipe your tears when you have fears,
But don't worry, baby, because Momma is always here.
I'll love you forever, no matter what.
Just remember, in the end, I'm the only one you can trust.
Hold on to your dreams and follow GOD's way,
Remember, GOD made your path for you to be successful
someday.

Smart, Beautiful, and Elegant

Smart, beautiful, and elegant too.
I'm so BLESSED to have a daughter as special as you.
You grow every day, and you have started to find your way.
I'm so very proud of you, baby, and don't know the right words
to say.
You try your best at everything you do, in hopes that one day
all your dreams will come true.
Hold your head up high and always look to the sky.
For GOD is always watching and smiling down on you.
You warm my heart, as for you have from the start.
As your mother, I hope we never grow apart.

Growing

Growing more and more every day.
It's hard being the perfect mother when you run out of the right things to say.
You're beautiful and smart and have always had my heart.
It's been a true blessing watching you grow from the start.
Keep believing and keep on achieving.
If you stick with me, never worry about me leaving.
I'll hold your hand when life gets tough,
But don't worry, it's not always rough.
I'll wipe your tears when you have fears,
But don't worry, baby, because Momma is always here
I'll love you forever no matter what.
Just remember, in the end, I'm the only one you can trust.
Hold on to your dreams and follow GOD's way,
Remember, GOD made your path for you to be successful someday.

I'll Love You Forever

I'll love you forever, no matter where you go.
I'll always be beside you as you continue to learn and grow.
I'll always support you in your dreams and goals.
I look forward to seeing where in life you will go.
I'll be you're biggest fan, just so you know.
Your dreams and aspirations are what warm my soul.

First Time I Held You In My Arms

First time I held you in my arms.
I knew you would always be my little lucky charm.
I knew I had to protect you and keep you from harm.
The first sight of danger would sound off my alarm.
I will fight to protect you and give my last arm.
For I will never let anyone cause you any harm.
You're my luck and my charm, and you will always have a
spot right here in Momma's arms.

A Daughter Is Like
Your Best Friend

A daughter is like your best friend.
When you're broken, she will help you amend.
She's like a rubber band that will never let you bend.
She will be there with you from the beginning to the end.
When you need a hand, she will give you hers to lend.
With her, you never have to pretend.
Your friendship with her will never suspend.
Your love for her will overextend.
There is no better person that I would recommend.

Mother's Day

"A Mother's love is more beautiful than any fresh flower."

- *Debasish Mridha*

Always Watching

For so many years, I wondered how you knew, just what we kids would always do. You always seemed to catch us in everything, too. Remember when I asked you, "Were you looking at me?" Now, I see GOD blessed you with double eyes
to always see not just me, but the whole family. We thank you
for all your love and support, we'd like to present this gift to help you keep a closer eye on all of us. We love you, Granny and
Mom, and we want you to see just how much you really mean.
Happy Mother's Day!!!!

Watching Over Me

Do you remember when I used to always ask you, "Are you looking at me?"
Well, now I see you were just watching over me.
We have our ups and our downs, even though sometimes you do make me frown.
But now I see you are the one who watches over me.
I love you, I do with all my heart, although sometimes things do fall apart.
But I still love you deep within my heart.

To: My Grandmother

Grandmother, Grandmother

Grandmother, grandmother, I can't tell you how much I
love you
like no other.
You're always there for me, and you love and care for me.
You're the person I'm always so excited to come and see.
You watch over me and never let me flee.
For I know, our love will always be.
You believe in me, and we will always be.
For when I'm feeling down, it's you I always see.
You stand by me and are always there, even from a
distance,
you're still with me.
I will always love you, whether here or there, even if I'm in
the
middle of nowhere.

Happy Mother's Day, Granny!!!

To: Granny (5-13-18)

M-O-T-H-E-R

M is for your motherly love.
O is for obvious GOD sent you from above.
T is for thankfulness for the mother GOD made just for me.
H is for your heart that gave me the love I need and made
me
the woman GOD wanted me to be.
E is for eternity, for my mother you will always be.
R is for respect because that's how you raised me to be.

Happy Mother's Day to a wonderful mother you turned out
to be.

To:
My Mom (3-14-16)

From The Day I Was Born

From the day I was born.
You always made sure I was never torn.
You held me tight to keep me from the evil and the fright.
You protected me from the dark and evil night.
When I grew older, you gave me a nightlight.
You were there by my side, and you never let me out of
sight.

The Gift of a Mother

A mother is full of love, that was a special gift from above. She loves so
much, it's hard to live without her gentle touch. She loves you and
cares for you, and one day she hopes you will see her through. Mothers
grow old and so does their soul, but it doesn't mean they stop loving you.
So take time out and do what your mother would do, one day she will
need you to carry her through.

To:
My Mom and Grandma (3-14-16)

You're My Heart

Mom, you're my heart,
Your love for me keeps me from falling apart.
I'm glad you've been on this journey with me from the
start.
You're the piece of the puzzle that makes living life the
best part.
Every day I thank GOD for giving me a mom with such a
huge
heart.
You hold the key that leads you to the inner me.
You're so special, and I want you to know, for your baby I
will
always be.
No, time is too short, no distance is too far; for where I'll be,
my
heart is where you always are.
I love you, Mom!!!!

To:
My Mother (4-29-18)

Father's Day

"Sometimes," said Pooh

"The smallest things
take up the most room
in your heart."

Happy Father's Day

The world is so big, the world is so huge.
Thank GOD, I've not had so many blues.
Not a dad in sight, but three wonderful uncles who raised
me just right.
One like my brother and my best friend, one who always
taught me
GOD's love will never end, and one who always made me
laugh and
sometimes cry.
Each one with a special gift, each one that has given me a
great lift.
My world would be empty without the three of you, for
GOD only knew just
how much I needed you.
Some people can't see just how much they mean to you
until you show
them that you really love them, too.
I've taken each lesson from each of you and applied it to
life in hopes of
turn out just like you raised me to do.
My life has been filled with joy, happiness, sadness, love,
and I'm still
thanking GOD for the wonderful Uncles He sent from
above. You may
not be my dad, but close enough, GOD sure knew what he
was doing
when he gave each of you a touch of love. You're fathers
now, and that's

just great, because your children will experience the love that some
people will never get to take.
I thank you all for the love you gave to me, and I want you to know I
love you all three.
To:
My Wonderful Uncles!

Valentine's Day

Happy Valentine's Day, Mom

Happy Valentine's Day to you.
Happy Valentine's Day, I love you.
Red, Pink, and White
You're the best mother in my sight.
I love you, I do, because you have always seen me through.
You will always be in my heart, even when things fall apart.

Happy Valentine's Day, Mom!!!!

To:
My Mom (2-12-16)

I Try To Live For You

I try to live for you, just like my mom did for me.
You don't understand now, but one day you will see.
You will understand that all I did was never for me.
You will see that no matter where you go, there I will always be.
My love surrounds you to show just how much you mean.
You will never be unnoticed or, better yet, unseen.
All these years to go, I'll be here, you just lean.
You never need a reason to come and talk to me, I'm always in the shadows, just look and you will see.
Forever my sweet girl and my baby you will always be.

Happy Valentine's Day, sweet girl!!

I love you to the stars and back

Religion/Spiritual

Dark Times

The darkness is here, but GOD calms our fear.
The light shines bright as Satan comes out in plain sight.
He prowls like a
serpent, but don't worry, GOD is here
because he knows the time is URGENT. So, open your eyes,
you shall see.
Don't be blind, because Satan is busy, and he will not flee.
We must fight and stay
strong, because he just doesn't belong, and wait for that
day for GOD to call us all
home.

True Colors

Red, Yellow, Black, or White
We are all the same in GOD's sight.
Each and every one of us shines so bright.
We just don't know how much GOD loves
us with all his might. The look, the touch, and
the feel, we all have our very own special appeal.
With all of our own secrets to reveal.

A Voice Called Out To Me

I heard a voice calling to me.
He said, "My child, where might you be?" He said, "Hiding
from me? Don't you know I can always see?"
I replied, "Yes, LORD." He said, "Now come on out and talk
to me. Whatever you say or
whatever you've done, don't fear, for I am your Father and
will always be.
Now wipe your tears and open your eyes, go on, child, I'm
right behind."
I said, "Thank you, LORD, for not letting me go blind."
He said, "I see your pain and frustration, too, but it's okay
because I believe in you. I see all the mess in the world, too.
No need to worry, for it will be time to come home soon."

A Rainbow After Every Storm

There is a rainbow after every storm.
It's the sign that the new world was born.
A reminder that the old was worn and torn.
It's something happy, and we don't have to mourn.
It's the day GOD let us be reborn.
Even though one day his son would have to be stuck with a thorn.

As I Lay Down My Head To Sleep

As I lay down my head to sleep,
I know the LORD is watching over me.
As I close my eyes, in the dark I'll see
I know the LORD will surround me.
As I start to fall into a deep sleep,
I know the LORD is here with me.
As I pray to the LORD my soul to keep,
I know he is always protecting me in my sleep.
As I sleep through the night, he holds me tight.
He keeps me from all the night fright.
As I wake up and see the sun,
I know it's the LORD's Will and it was done,
For another day has begun.

He Will Guide Us Where We Go

He will guide us where we go.
He is the only one to know.
He will always tell us so.
His love for us will always flow.
He will sometimes tell us no.
His precious blood saved our souls.
He will always shine and glow.
His time will never ever be slow.
His love for us will always grow.

Rainbow

The rainbow is beautiful all the way through.
It starts with red, orange, yellow, indigo, and ends
in blue. All the colors that GOD created
are just for me and you. The rainbow was a
promise GOD made to see us all through. He made
the promise not to flood the earth, like he did in
Noah's Day. So, when you see a rainbow, look up
and say, "Thank you, LORD, for your Saving Grace
and for giving us another day."

Calling My Name

Softly, calmly calling my name.
You're my Savior and the world's fame.
The world needed you, and you came.
You took the persecution and all the blame.
Your love means more than all fame.
You're the only one who can beat Satan at his game.
Thank you, LORD, for loving us so.
Thank you, LORD, for giving up your soul.
You did exactly what you were told.
You saved so many, and most will never know.
Your Love and Blessings will always flow.
You shed your blood just so we would know.

Come To Me

Come to me today, I will help you and lead you on your way.
I will overlook your sin and love you deep down from within.
I will undo your wrongs and help you make them right.
I will forever keep you in my sight.
No matter where you always are,
I will be with you near and far.

For I Walk Through The Valley

For I walk through the valley of the shadow of death, I shall fear no evil.
For you are always watching and protecting me.
For no matter where evil will be, I know you're near, surrounding me.
For when it is dark, and I cannot see, your light is what will guide me.
For when I fear what evil may be, I look up and your face I will see.
I know the dark shadows may follow me.
But with your protection, you will make them flee.
I know that evil will always be, but because I'm your child, SATAN can never have me.

He Lives

He lives, so we can face today.
He lives, so we can face tomorrow.
He lives, so one day there will be no pain or sorrow.
He lives because there is still faith and hope to borrow.
He lives because he died to set us free.
He lives because his love will always be.

He's Coming On A Cloud

He's coming in on a cloud.
Listen carefully because the trumpet will be loud.
It will surely draw in a large crowd.
When he sees all of his children, he will be very proud.
He will gather all the Christians, for they are the only ones allowed.
He will come and meet us as he vowed.
At his arrival, we will all be wowed.

I Heard A Voice Call Out to Me

I heard a voice call out to me,
He said, "My child, I'm glad you can finally see.
Lost in the dark and fallen by sin."
He said, "My child, come walk with me, and I'll guide you
from within. Fear not, no more, for I'm here,
my love, always watching over you from up above.
Go in peace and remember me, for if you ever need me,
you'll know where I'll be.
Satan is busy, but so am I; if he bothers you, I'll make him
flee."

I Know Not Where
You Will Lead Me

For I know not where you will lead me, but I know you will
need to see just what kind of
woman you want me to be.
For this world will not accept me for free, but I know you
will stand and make my
plea.
For everything is always around and ready to be seen, but I
know you will make evil
flee.
For the world will not always see the kind of woman you
want me to be.
That's why I come to you down on one knee, praying you
will always look down and
protect me.

I Know Not The Day
Nor The Hour

For I know not the day, nor the hour when you will come for me.
I plan to be ready for wherever I will be.
For the sound of the trumpet or the Angel, I will see.
Wherever I will be, I will be ready for thee.
For when you come, I will finally be pain-free.
I will know you're near when all my worries flee.
I will bow on one knee as I PRAISE thee.
For when my time has come, you're all I will see.

I Look For Your Face

I look for your face everywhere, yet it's so hard to find.
I know it's not meant to be seen yet, because it would
cause me to go blind.
I look high into the mountains and down into the valley
and out across the sea.
Where I feel your spirit walking in front, behind, and beside
me.
My journey would be hard, and my life would fall apart, if it
wasn't for your Grace and
Mercy.
You said that times would be tough, but nothing for you is
too rough.
Your face is everywhere, it's here, it's there, it's in the air.
We just must trust that you're always there.
I walk by FAITH and not by sight, I trust in you for you're
my light.

I Pray That You Will Guide Me

LORD, I pray that you will guide me on my way.
LORD, I pray that you will help me not stray.
LORD, I pray that you will be with me each day.
LORD, I pray that with me you will always stay.
LORD, I pray that you will help me know your way.
LORD, I pray that you will strengthen me all the way.
LORD, I pray that you will be with me when I sway.
LORD, I pray that you will always tell me what to say.
I may not always know or always do right, but I know no
matter where I go, I will always
be in your sight.
No matter where I go, or how dark the road is, I know you'll
always
protect me with all
your strength and might.
The road may be rough and the journey may be long, but I
know with your help I'll have
the strength to fight.
So, keep me by your side and never let me go, for my
FAITH I'll always hold onto with
all my might.

I See You In The Daylight And Hear You At Night

I can see you in the daylight and hear you in the night.
I know you're always with me, and there is no need to be
afraid. You always lead my way because you're my light.
I hear your voice in times of need and know everything will
be alright. When things get tough and
look rough, you always hold me tight. I know you're always
protecting me and fighting evil with
all your might. No matter where I go or where I am, you
will always be in my sight.
I will follow you
all the way through and know you'll guide me right. I will
no longer be afraid of the bumps in the
night because I know for me you'll always shine your light.

I Set Out On A Journey

I set out on a journey many years ago.
Hoping I could find the answers that you would only know.
I got lost a few times around, but you reached down and
pointed me in the direction I
should go.
You told me no need to rush, this journey had to be
traveled slow.
If I stayed straight and didn't sway, I would make my way
to finally see your face glow.
You will follow me until the road ends, and your love will
continue to flow.
You'll carry me from midair to the GOLDEN GATES and the
man upstairs, for this
I surely know.
For there we will meet and my answers He will show.
Most of them will be obsolete, because now there is no
need to know.
For I will have found the place where I was to go, and there
my journey will have
ended so.
I know from here until the end your love will continue to
grow.
You will follow me from here until the end, until you finally
take my soul.

I'm Standing
In The Need Of Prayer

Lord, I'm standing here in need of Prayer.
Hoping you can hear me up there.
Life is short and not always fair.
Some people down here just don't care.
Sometimes, life is like playing truth or dare.
Sometimes, your cupboards may end up bare.
Some people wake up with nothing to wear.
But I know you will provide even from way up there.
Sometimes, I just look to the sky and sit and stare, often
wondering what you do up there.
Lord, I'm standing in need of Prayer.
Hoping you can find just a moment to spare.
I have so much I need to share.
Soon, I will meet you in midair.

Invest In The BIBLE

Invest in the BIBLE, it's reliable. Everything in it is so undeniable. The stories are real, and you can see everything GOD chose to reveal. From creation to the end, see how things will amend. The stories keep going, they never end, for it's still going as GOD finalizes the end. He lines the Christians up to prepare for battle, as Satan and his demons' tails start to shake and rattle. Don't worry, we the CHRISTIANS will WIN the battle.

Lead Me To Your Way

Walk with me, LORD,
Lead me to your way.
For every day is a struggle, and on my own, I always sway.
Talk to me, LORD, and let me hear what you have to say.
Help me to block everything, LORD, so I can only see your
way.
For my battles are fierce and my heart is growing weak, I
need
you on this battlefield every single day.

Let The Sunshine

Let the sunshine, let it shine high. Let the day grow, until it's time for the moon to show. The birds sing until it's time for what the night will bring. Let the waters pour, as the beautiful eagles soar. Let the grass grow as the seasons come fast and slow. Let the flowers bloom, as spring continues to make room. GOD's beautiful creations are the best, and he knows better than the rest. Let the creator have his art because one day men will fall apart.

Lighthouse

You're my lighthouse when in need.
The only safe place I want to be.
You shine your light for me to see.
When it's dark, there you will forever be.
When lost at sea, your light finds me.
I'm so thankful for your lighthouse
That always saves me.
Dark at night, light at day, your lighthouse
Will always help me to find my way.

LORD, I Am Weak And You're Strong

LORD, for I am weak and you're strong.
LORD, help me find where I belong.
You told me this journey would be long.
You said you would follow me all along.
LORD help me to know right from wrong.
I will praise you, LORD, as I sing your song.

LORD, do not let me fall, for I am weak.
For it is I that Satan will seek.
For I can't afford my FAITH to leak.
For if I do, he will know I'm weak.
He will think I'm not strong, and I'm mild and meek.
He will not hide, for me he will seek.
Comfort me, LORD, and protect me from him.
For if you're with me, he will flee.

Lord Help Me

She cried out, "LORD, please help me." He said, "Hold on, my dear child, for you're not lost, you've just been found." He said, "You were blind, but now that you've been touched, you'll see just fine." He said, "When you call on me, it will always be my love and guidance you will find. When you're in fear, just remember, my child, it's my voice you will always hear. So, don't be scared for the word has been shared, and I will never let you go. Continue to hold on, and never let go, for if not, Satan will try to pull you down below. So never fear, for I am always here, and I love you more than you will ever know.

Lord, It's Me

Lord, it's me, it's me, standing in need of Prayer.
Lord, someone out there has their cupboards bare.
I'm standing in need of Prayer.
Lord, someone out there has nothing to wear.
I'm standing in need of Prayer.
Lord, someone out there wants to no longer care.
I'm standing in need of Prayer.
Lord, the world nowadays doesn't play fair.
I'm standing in need of Prayer.
Lord, someone out there has no love to share.
I'm standing in need of Prayer.

LORD, You Comfort Me

LORD, you comfort me all through the day.
LORD, you're always telling me the right things to say.
LORD, you guide me to follow you and your way.
Whenever I feel down and blue, I bow to you and Pray.
I say, thank you, LORD, for always guiding me and helping me not to sway.
I'll always know no matter what, you'll never let me stray.
No matter how far I go, you'll never go away.
No matter where life leads me, you are the one I will obey.

My LORD and Savior

You're my LORD and Savior.
My needs are always met.
You're always standing with me and beating Satan at his bet.
You will never leave me and never will forget.
You're my LORD and Savior.
You haven't let me down yet.
You comfort me and love me.
For I will always see.
I know not to ask if you have forsaken me.
I know you're always with me and teaching me to do my best.
When things get too tough, you even let me rest.
I will forever follow you and never leave your nest.

Shining Way Up High

I see you shining way up high.
I feel your rain drop way down low.
I love the way you make the wind blow.
I wonder how you make the seasons change fast and slow.
Your lightning strikes and makes the sky glow.
But you always send the rainbow to let us know,
You're still up there loving us and letting it show.
We thank you for beauty and your creation, but most of all,
we thank you for loving and
caring for us so.
We are thankful to have a FATHER who we will always
know.

Show Me Your Way, O' LORD

Show me your way, O' LORD.
Show me how to be.
Show me how to love others, the same way you love me.
Show me your way, O' LORD.
Show me how to see.
Show me how to see the world in the way you wanted it to be.
Show me your way, O' LORD.
Show me how to be free.
Show me how you died for me and didn't charge a fee.
Show me your way, O' LORD.
Show me the way to thee.
Show me how to get to Calvary, where it was all meant to be.
Your love will always steadily hold and will always be the same.
I thank you, LORD, for allowing me to always call upon your name.
I praise you, LORD, each day and for showing me your way.
I think you, LORD, for picking me up when I always start to sway.

Stormy Day

The clouds are grey, the clouds roll in.
This is what it looks like on a stormy day.
The winds roar, and raindrops fall.
There is never a storm for GOD that is too small.
The wind is chill, but there is still a warm feeling
GOD will soon say, "Peace, be still."

The Blood He Shed

He shed his blood for me.
He shed his blood to set me free.
He died upon the cross to save me from my loss.
He wiped my tears away and said, "I'll be back for you some day."
His name is Yeshua, and for us, he paid the price.

Your Rod Has Struck Me

Your rod has struck me a time or two.
For sinful things that I do.
But without your discipline and love, too, I wouldn't know
what direction to go in.
Your love for me is what gets me through.
That's why every day I praise you.
I look to the sky and bow before you, for I have so much
love I want to show you.

The Clouds Are Grey

The clouds are grey, the clouds roll in.
This is what it looks like on a stormy day.
The winds roar, and raindrops fall.
There is never a storm for GOD that is too small.
The wind is chill, but there is still a warm feeling.
GOD will soon say Peace be still.

The Darkness of The World

In the darkness of the world,
I feel evil trying to fight.
No longer scared of the light,
Evil no longer visits just at night,
It comes out even in broad daylight.
I still see your light shining bright.
Evil only fears with you in sight.
We need your love with all your might to help us win
Satan's fight.

The Price He Paid

His name is Yeshua.
He died on the cross for me.
He is the reason I believe.
He died to set me free.
I believe he rose from the dead.
I chose to follow him instead.
He paid the price for me,
When the bright red blood was shed.

The Storm Is Coming

The storm is coming, be ready for it. For if you are
not careful, he will snag thee. For his demons are
lined up and ready for battle, as their snakeskin and
tails are starting to rattle. He has no fear and never
sheds a tear. For Satan is his name and evil is his
game. He is faster than a cheetah, more venomous
than a poison dart frog, and sly as a fox, and can
hide easily under big or small rocks. We have to
fight strong and hard and keep putting up our
defensive blocks. For he knows we are coming and can't
be protected by his rocks. He is busy as a bee,
and knows his time will be. But GOD's Grace and
Mercy are what will make him flee.

The World Is Mad

This world has gotten oh so mad.
You can't turn on the news because it's mostly bad.
There are so many situations that are so sad.
Many people are ungrateful for what they had.
Some people are worried about what's the new fad.
People have forgotten how to be glad.
We forget about the war in places like Baghdad.
While there are people walking around with no Mom or
Dad.
What happened to the world to make it so mad? Why
aren't people still oh so glad?
Evil will continue to add and add, it doesn't matter how
the situation is or how sad.
Satan stops at nothing because he is bad. He likes seeing
the whole world being torn
and mad.

Walk With Me, Lord

Walk with me, LORD,
be my battle sword,
For Satan is busy and buzzing like a bee.
Walk with me, LORD,
help me see
the perfect way to defeat him.
Walk with me, LORD,
for he is strong,
but with your help
I know he will not last long.
Walk with me, LORD,
to help me fight the battle.
For soon Satan's snake tail
will stop with the rattle.
Walk with me, LORD,
help me to fight,
defend me with your
shield, LORD, and protect me
with all your might.
Walk with me, LORD,
as we win this victory,
for your Grace and Mercy will always be.

Your Rainbow
Is The Color Of Love

For your rainbow is the color of love.
It always shines from high up above.
Each color is so beautiful and bright.
Each feeding off your beautiful sunlight.
It's a sign of your protection and will to fight,
To make sure each and every one of us is always alright.
It lets us know that even at night, there is always a source
of some type of light.
That even a gloomy day can have a beautiful sight.

You're A Light Unto My Path

You're a light unto the world, a guide to a path.
You're the one people seek when they see the great wrath.
We will follow your footpath, as you lead us away from the warpath.
We will march into victory as we steer clear of Satan's bloodbath.
There will be hearts broken and souls lost due to the aftermath.
There will be hope again when they see you standing in front of the path.

From Above

He shines His light from high above.
To rain down on us His perfect love.
From daylight up to sunlight down, He looks down on us
and sometimes will
frown.
No matter what, He still sends His love down, to let us
know He will not always
frown.
Happy or not, He still shines His light, from morning sun
and the moonlight.
It shines so bright from day to night, to show us how much
He loves us with all His
might.

His Creation

He created this beautiful universe, but today it's
getting worse.
It's not a play or a book, so no, it's not been rehearsed.
It's the sound of evil that's putting on the curse.
The only thing to save us is His Bible verse.
Satan is busy, and he will not flee, the only way
To fix it is send GOD a plea. He crawls around
And doesn't make a sound, waiting to prey on the
One's lost and not found. He's scared of light,
Because he's an awful sight. Because when
God shines his light, Satan knows he has lost his last fight.

Lost and Found

She said, "I was lost, but now I'm found. God saved me
before I
almost drowned.
I once was blind, but GOD entered my mind, now I can
see, since
He's
Set me free. It's amazing, the things GOD has done for me.
He
saved me
From Satan and helped me flee. All I had to do was send
GOD a
plea,
to reach down and save a wretch like me."

At The Cross

There at the cross is where Jesus saved us from
our loss. His blood was shed, and it was bright
and red. He suffered and died for us instead.
He said, "Father, why have you forsaken me?"
But he knew the LORD would never let him be,
especially when he gave his life for you and me.
He hung on tight and fought with all his might,
until he hung his head, and that's when we
knew he took his last breath. He died to set us
free, even though he knew Satan still wouldn't
let us be. But he knew with blood, we would
still be safe from him.

Thankfulness

Thank you, GOD, for the food.
Thank you, GOD, for being you.
Thank you, GOD, for my family, too.
Thank you, GOD, for your love.
Thank you, GOD, for your son from above.
Thank you, GOD, for providing us with what we are deprived of.
Thank you, GOD, for watching from above.

You're With Us Every Day

You're with us every day.
You're with us when we pray.
No matter what people say
You're the one who guides our way.
If we follow you, we shall never sway.

Your Voice In The Night

I hear your voice in the night.
Saying, don't fear, my child, sleep tight.
I see you from above and you're alright.
For you know, my child, you're always in my sight.
Close your eyes and you will be just fine.
For I am with you and will not let evil cross the line.
You're safe in the night and never have a reason to have a fright.
Remember, my child, I'm always your light.
Just call out my name and I'll hold you tight.

Upon His Face

Amazing Grace was upon His face as He bled upon the cross.
The blind could see and the lost were found as He died and bled for thee.
He cried out loud, "LORD, why have you forsaken me?"
But He rose again on day three to make his final plea.
The blood He shed was out of love, and He died to set us free.

I Couldn't Become
Who I Am Today

I couldn't have become who I am today.
For you are my GOD and you made me in my own special
way.
For you are the one I pray to from day to day.
You help me stay straight and not sway.
I follow your lead and try to obey.
Even when I go astray, you always lead me back your way.
I know you're here to always stay and will never ever go
away.

This Is My Story, This Is My Song

This is my story; this is my song.
You've been by my side all along.
When I was weak, you helped me to be strong.
You showed me just where I belong.
For you have never once left me alone.
Your love is the best I've ever known.
You're the reason my FAITH has grown.
Your love for me has always shone.

When It's Dark And Gloomy

When it's dark and gloomy and I need your light,
I wait for you to shine it down and tell me everything's alright.
I know that I can come out of hiding and regain sight.
There is nothing left to be afraid of, and I know you will hold me tight.
I can relax and know there is no reason to be afraid.
With you, everything is always just right; it gives me peace to sleep at night.
Thank you, LORD, for protecting me with all your might.

I See Your Footprints In Front Of Me

I see your footprints in front of me.
That's how I know you carried me.
In pain and suffering, you were with me.
You never left me alone or let me be.
When I was lost, you found me.
When I was blind, you helped me see.
When I was sad, you comforted me.
When I was sick, you nursed me.
Thank you, LORD, for carrying me.
Thank you for letting your love always be.
I'm so glad you saved a wretch like me.

This Journey Is Long And Narrow Too

This journey is long and narrow too.
But I know I can trust you to guide me through.
I only want to follow you.
Things will get tough, and the path will get rough.
But I know, with you, your protection is enough.
There will be good and some bad, but you will be there
In times even when I'm sad.
You will take away my anger when I get mad, you will
protect me when things start to get bad.
I chose you as my LORD and Savior, and for that I will
always be glad.

I See Changes
In The Sun And Moon

I see the changes in the sun and the moon
I see the weather is changing, too.
I know these are signs that you're coming soon.
I'm excited to know you're taking us with you.

The animals keep disappearing, and more natural
Disasters keep appearing.
The scientists are really starting to look weary.
They wonder why everything is so dreary.

We skip over spring and go straight into the heat
Some people are still lost, because things are no longer
neat.
The funny part is the weatherman can no longer compete.
The weather maps they show are always beat.
Nothing they say makes any sense, you turn the TV on
And it's like everything is on repeat.

Evil is on the rise, and listening to the news is no longer
Like "Oh Surprise." People are crazy and becoming very
lazy. Trying to figure out if the world is really ending? Yes,
no, or maybe?
There is so much darkness, most can't see the light.
They have been blinded for too long and lost their sight.

The Enemy Is Not
Who We Can See

The enemy is not who we can see.
The enemy is the one who goes unseen.
Hiding behind his big smoke screen.
Hoping people can't see that he is truly careless and mean.
He is always causing chaos on the scene.
Always leaving a mess and everything unclean.
Always somewhere fleeing on the scene, in hopes that he
can stay hidden and unseen.

Remember, the enemy is not the one you can see.
The enemy is the one who invisibly battles you and me.
His name is Satan, and he will always be,
Walking around trying to scare you and me.
Forgetting how GOD saved us, he forgets that one day
GOD will finally make him flee.

Causing All The Trouble Everywhere You Go

Causing all the trouble everywhere you go,
You're always breaking and taking someone's precious soul.
Trying to brainwash them and take the good that they know.
You always leave them empty and lying low.
You always get excited when their love stops to flow.
You love to see when their soul has lost its shimmering, shiny glow.
Taking the life from them, harsh and slow.
You find it enjoyable because for you it's all a show.
Just remember, GOD looks down on us here below.
Never letting you truly take that person's beautiful soul.
You can try all you want, but just so you know,
GOD's love is always flowing down and will always shine and glow.
He will protect us from all the evil things you want so bad for us to know

He Died Upon The Cross

He died upon the cross.
He gave his life for me.
He is the only Savior I praise, for I lift my hands to thee.
The blood he shed was bright and red, but he paid the price so we could all be free.
For he rose again on day three, for all the world to see.
For one day, he will come again, and from Satan we will finally flee.

He Has Risen From The Dead

He has risen from the dead.
He died and rose again.
He saved us from our sin.
His blood left stains upon His skin.
He hung His head, but had FAITH deep within.
He died upon the cross, so a new change would begin.
He said He would follow us from start to end.
He is our LORD and Savior and a good friend.
When you stand with Him, you never have to pretend.
He gave his life for us to make amends.

Last Call Home

The curtains are almost closing, the end is almost near.
He's only calling once, so make sure your ears are clear.
The final act is approaching, watch the news, and you will hear.
The world is now trembling in nothing but pain and fear. The saints are already preparing to fight the evil that is here.
The weather is always changing, it's no longer a good atmosphere.
Don't you hear Him calling? His voice is loud and clear.
The train is approaching, the last call home is almost here.
Listen for the trumpet, for it will only sound for certain ears.

People Will Disappear

People will disappear right before your eyes.
Be careful who you follow, you might be in for a big
surprise.
The World is always watching, but never taking His advice.
Jesus said He was coming, and to be ready would be wise.
Be ready today or even tomorrow, because soon the skies
will open and there He will rise.
If you're sleeping when He arrives, you might get left and
not realize.
For He will appear in the clouds right before our very eyes.

Baby/Kids Poems

Doesn't Matter, I Will Love You

Pink or blue, no matter what, I will love you.
Girl or boy, no matter what, you will always be my joy.
Nine months of waiting, while we are eagerly
anticipating what to name the baby, my heart beats as I
can't wait to feel your
feet.
That's when I will know my world will be complete. So,
take your time and grow,
fast or slow. I'll be here when you're ready, no matter how
things go.
I'll always be your mother, just to let you know.

Be Careful, Little Feet, Where You Go

Oh, be careful, little feet, where you go. For there is danger
in the world and places that
will surely lead you so.
Oh, be careful, little eyes, what you see. For the world may
not always look as it seems
to be.
Oh, be careful, little ears, what you hear. For everything
might not always sound so
pretty and clear.
Oh, be careful, little mouth, what you say. For one day, it
might cause you to disobey.
Oh, be careful, little hands, what you touch. For some
things might feel pretty rough.
Oh, be careful, little heart, what you love. For not all things
come from above.
Oh, be careful, little body, what you do. For you should
never let anyone touch you.
For there is a Father up above, and He is looking down
with love. He will always be here
to protect you.
To the Children of the World.

As I Lay Down
My Head To Sleep

As I lay down my head to sleep,
I know the LORD is watching over me.
As I close my eyes, for dark I'll see
I know the LORD will surround me.
As I start to fall into a deep sleep,
I know the LORD is here with me.
As, I Pray to the LORD my soul to keep,
I know he is always protecting me in my sleep.
As, I sleep through the night, he holds me tight.
He keeps me from all the night fright.
As, I wake up and see the sun.

I know it's the LORDS will and it was done,
For another day has begun.

Rockabye Baby

Rockabye baby, it's time for night-night.
When you wake up, I'll be holding you tight.
When you open your eyes, you will see the morning light.
You will be so happy to see a beautiful sight.

Rockabye baby, it's time for night-night.
No need to worry, for I will protect you with all my might.
Go to sleep, baby, no bad dreams to fight.
For when you wake up, you will see GOD's beautiful light.

LORD, Take This Child And Love Them

LORD, take this child and love them with all your might.
LORD, take this child and hold them tight.
When they go out into the world, LORD, guide them with your light.
Protect this child, LORD, and always keep them in your sight.
Thank you, LORD, for protecting them from the fight.
When they lie down, LORD, I know they're safe at night.
With your protection, LORD, they will always be alright.

Baby In The Tub

Scrub a dub dub, baby in the tub.
Playing with toys and having some fun.
Bubbles are growing, and the baby is spit blowing.
The little yellow duck is swimming around, while Momma
and baby make funny sounds.
Time to get clean, the baby knows what that means.
Time to get out, and the baby starts to scream and pout,
until Momma holds the baby and turns the lights out.
She sings a lullaby and kisses the baby goodnight, as the
baby closes their eyes and snuggles up tight.
As it's finally time to say night-night.

3-16-16

Grief

Mom, I Miss You

Mom, I miss you so, but I know it was your time to go.
I know if I look, I will still see you in my shadow.
The pain is hard to bear, and the tears still flow.
I know GOD only took you because He was ready for your soul.
So, rest assured that I am fine, but the healing will be slow.
If I just look around, I can still see your love show.
I know you're now watching me down below, just know I miss you, Mom, and I will see you again as soon as the trumpet blows.

In Memory of Mom (Granny) 5-15-20
From all your kids:

LORD, When You Came To Get Me

LORD, when you came to get me, you said, My child, it's time to go. Now close your
eyes and hold on tight and breathe really slow. No need to hurry because where we
are going is a place you already know. Follow me and listen to my voice, for the Angels
will soon show. To guide you home and to the Golden Gate that will open for you slow.
There I'll meet you and take your hand, and you will see HEAVEN as it will glow.
You'll take your wings and be pain-free, for now you're home with me.
You're finally home and now can see HEAVEN is exactly what I said it would be.
Fear not, my child, for you will reign forever high up here with me.
So, open your eyes and enjoy, for it's all for you to see.

In Memory of a Dear Friend

Not So Clear

Now you're gone and I'm still here.
Life is sad and not so clear.
There are days I still shed a tear, but I remember when you
told me there is nothing to fear.
You said you were ready and were loud and clear.
Sometimes, your voice is all I still hear.

You're safe and in the highest place.
I'm still down here trying to make sense of your empty
space.
I know life goes on, but thank GOD, I still have visions of
your lovely face.

In Memory of Dear Friend

Sometimes I Forget That You're No Longer Here

Sometimes I forget that you're no longer here.
I remember it like it was yesterday when you had to disappear.
I knew you were ready and had no fear.
But that didn't stop me from shedding a tear.
I know you're okay, because your voice I can still hear.
I still see you in my visions, constantly trying to wipe away my tears.

You always told me you would be here,
I always wondered, even if you weren't near.
But now I know you show up in my dreams and help take away my fear.
GOD has called and brought you home, but not to leave your loved ones all alone.
Our hearts may feel empty, but our love is still strong.
We go on missing you all year long.

In Memory of #70

I See Your Face
On My Weak Days

I see your face on my weak days.
I hear your voice always.
It's so hard facing life without you.
But, if you were here, I know what you would do.
You would wipe my tears and hold my hand and tell me
this is something I can get through.
You would look at me and tell me to be strong, too.
You would tell me it may not be easy living without you,
but it's something you know I can do.
I try to pick up the pieces and keep on going because
down here life keeps on flowing.
I miss you more every day and never know what to say.
My love for you is still put away, and I can't wait to see you
again someday.

In Memory of a Dear Friend

Every Day I Feel Your Presence By My Side

Every day I feel your presence by my side
As I always have tears I try and hide.
For so many years, all I've done is cried.
I feel like I have to let time slide and put the
Pain and hurt aside.
I wish our time hadn't gone by.
Some days, I still ask the question, Why?
I wish I could look up and see your face in the sky.
Every day is hard, but all I can do is try.
It's never easy saying goodbye.

The Sirens Still Go

The sirens still go, but I know you will not show.
The lights still go on, but I know you're forever gone.
Sometimes when I hear the sirens sound, I feel that's when
you're looking down.
Time has not stopped, but our hearts have stood still.
But they beat again, when we know you're with God in a
heaven that is real.

In Memory of #70  !!!
3-7-16

Looking Down From Up Above

Looking down from up above.
I still send down my wonderful love.
I know the pain will not go away,
But trust me, I am now finally okay.
It's hard to believe I am no longer here.
It's okay, have no fear.
My pain and suffering have disappeared.
I know there are days you still wish I were here,
But GOD called me early, because He needed me near.
He told me He would wipe your face when you shed a tear.
Have no fear, your time will come near, and I'll meet you
again someday, waiting right here.

In Memory of a Dear Friend (Sweet Angel RIP)

Here Today, Gone Tomorrow

Here today, gone tomorrow.
Don't worry about me, I have no more pain or sorrow.
Don't be sad, just think of the time we had to borrow.
I know the tears are hard to swallow, but GOD called me
home and I had to follow.
Don't let the pain linger and wallow.
Grieve for me today, but move on tomorrow.
For GOD gave us all the time we needed to borrow.

Far Above The Light Blue Sky

Far above the light blue sky, you're looking down from way up high.
Looking down to Earth below, still sending down your perfect love.
Checking in to say hello, still hard sometimes to have to let go.
Never forgetting how I loved you so.
I loved you more than you will ever know.
It's still hard to believe we have lost your soul.
The time is gone, but the memories still flow.

Sometimes I See Your Sweet Face

Sometimes, I see your sweet face, still drifting in your empty space.
I know you're in a better place, but that doesn't make your spot easier to replace.
I miss seeing your smiling face, but I can only imagine what it's like being in GOD's Grace.
Every day I look for a trace that will help me fill your empty space.
After all these years, there is still no one special who can be put in your place.
I thank GOD for all the memories that I can still chase.

In Memory Of a Dear Friend

You Never Said Goodbye

You never said goodbye, you never said I have to go.
It only took a second for GOD to let us know.
You have gained your wings to fly, and as you soared and flew high.
Your new home was waiting, and GOD was, too. Don't worry, we will see you again really soon.
We know you're safe with him above, and he will still send us a touch of your amazing love.

In Memory of a good friend

People Are Dying All Around

People are dying all around.
Our love still surrounds and may never drown.
We feel the emptiness as we finally lay them down.
But knowing GOD is with them will help us not to frown.
They are now in Heaven and have finally received their crown.
We no longer have to worry, because they are now looking down.
In a better place where they will never have to frown.

Another Year Gone By

Another year gone by and many more to go.
It's still hard to believe that six years ago, GOD took your
precious soul.
Every day goes by and we still miss you so.
It's hard to say goodbye, even when you don't always
know.
The passing seems so sudden, but the time to heal is slow.
Our love for you will never fade; it will only continue to
grow.
So, every year may come and go, but our tears continue to
flow.
We thank GOD every day for loving you and taking your
precious soul.

In Memory Of A Good Friend

Just Yesterday

I just saw you yesterday and that pretty smile upon your face.
But today, GOD took your hand, because he had a better plan and said, "Come on, my child, it's time to go home to your new place."
It will take a while to get used to what is now your empty space.
I live in peace knowing you're now gone and in God's Grace.
I will always cherish all the memories, for those I will always be able to trace.
My heart is already beating, like I have run the longest race.
I know GOD will help me slow my heart back to the right pace.

In Memory Of Your Sweet Mother
RIP 7-18-19

I Miss You

I miss you dearly, I miss you yearly.
Ever since you've been gone, life has been quite dreary.
You used to tell me that you couldn't wait until the day
you met the LORD face-to-face.
I often wonder what it is like, but I know it was awesome
when you saw him eye-to-eye.
Even though sometimes we still wonder why, deep down
inside we know it was time.
GOD took you gently in his arms and took you away from
Earth's harm.
We know you're happy, safe, and free, and we can't wait to
see how wonderful HEAVEN will be.

In Memory Of A Dear Friend

3-17-16

You Saw The Light

You closed your eyes and saw the light.
You saw GOD's face, shiny and bright.
You knew it was time to go, time to finally give GOD your
precious soul.
You knew you didn't want to turn back, for you knew what
lay upon the old track.
You wanted to stay because you knew it was finally your
special day.
Although friends and family wish you could've stayed.
You're happy and free, and GOD called you up as His
angel-to-be.
The pain is over, you've been set free, GOD's Grace and
Mercy will help us see how much better you're with Him.

In Memory Of A Dear Friend

3-23-16

Domestic Violence

He Tried To Silence Me

He tried to silence me years ago.
Now, I've let the whole world know.
His secret is no longer not for show.
Now, I can actually let my face glow.
No longer hiding behind the shadow.
It took some time, and I came out slow.
No reason to hide from that dark shadow.
I'm ready to come out and let myself show.

6-29-18

Looking In The Mirror

Looking in the mirror, watching the old scars fade away.
I see my new face and spirit coming into play.
I no longer run from your shadow array.
I no longer worry about the hateful things you would say.
I no longer worry about you being in my way.
I wake up happy and go about my day.
No longer caring if you think it's not okay.

I am free and can finally be me.
I can look in the mirror and finally see.
I start to see the Woman GOD wants me to be.
I no longer have to wonder how do I flee.
It feels great being happy and being able to be free.
I'm so finally glad I got back to the true me.

She Wore A Mask
For Many Years

She wore a mask for many years, but it didn't really hide away all the fears.
This mask only hid all the pain and tears.
She looks in the mirror for the mark that always appears.
Hoping she doesn't have to show it to her closest peers.
She will hide behind the mask until time nears, until she can finally look in the mirror and see that it all clears. She is no longer hearing those horrible words she always hears.
She can now look in the mirror and see no more makeup smears.
She can then smile and be rid of all those horrible fears.
For the monster is gone and she will not have to shed any more tears.

I Hid My Face, I Hid My Heart

I hid my face, I hid my heart.
So many days, I didn't know where to start.
I would look in the mirror and walk away,
Not happy with the reflection that it gave.
I wanted to crawl and hide in a cave.
This relationship was like riding a wave.
Hoping one day I wouldn't see my grave,
that one day soon I would become happy and brave.

I Was Hidden In A Dark Place

I was hidden in a dark place, when my identity no longer matched my face.

It's hard to go out in the light when at home you have your own battle to fight.

You can always run but never truly hide. For your face will always tell the little white lie.

You tried to stay hidden, but you know deep within you really want people to see why you have been hiding.

A call for help, but most don't know you've been hurt all along, you just never let it show.

We Are Fragile

We are fragile and very thin; you can't break our surface or penetrate the skin.
Soft and gentle is the best touch, but careful we don't like it too rough.
Play with our hair or rub our backs, but just remember we don't like smacks.
Pick us up carefully and hold us real tight, just remember we are not your boys and don't want to fight.
Careful what you say, because we females sometimes take it another way.
It's good to take it slow, if you don't want to see us go.
We loved to be snuggled, kissed, and hugged.
But remember, we are fragile and don't need to be tugged.

The Scars Didn't Fade

The pain went away, but the scars didn't fade.
The memories are still fresh, like it happened yesterday.
The words still carry, because they were all you used to say.
I thought one day I could wake up and finally be on my way,
But the flashbacks still happen like it was just the other day. It's like trying to escape the mysterious corn maze.
It only happens here and there, the memories come just like a phase.
I'm still in shock to this day; I never thought it would happen, I'm still in amaze.

The Scars Never Faded

The scars may have faded, but the memories never went
away.
It's the pain I had to live through day by day.
Trying to hide the pain and fear in every single way.
There was never a day that the feelings didn't sway.
Not realizing they would always stay.
Looking in the mirror, wishing I could have hid from that
day, but sad to say it's how I got this way.
Taking my identity and trying to make me obey, whoever
told you this was ever OKAY?

I Look In The Mirror

I look in the mirror, and what do I see?
No longer the same person that I used to be.
I stare in the glass and wonder what happened to the old me.
Someone long ago stole my identity.
I will never be the me that I was before because I was broken and now trying to become much more.
Picking up the pieces to try and find me, I never realized just how hard it would be.
I look and I want to see the same old me, but all I see are the broken pieces I used to be.

Living In The Darkness

Living in the darkness, with barely any light.
Always hiding, trying to stay out of sight.
That's just how you liked it, so you could always fight.
Never caring that what you were doing wasn't even right.
Always making sure the relationship stayed tight.
Never seeing the tears that were shed at night.
All you cared about was no one seeing this horrible sight.

Gentle

She said, "Be gentle, because once things turned out accidental."
That was a day that turned out to be eventful. She said, "Love me right, but don't hold me too tight because the last time that happened it turned into a fight.
It caused me quite the fright." She said, "Care for me, but please don't flee, long ago that's how things turned out to be."
She said, "Love me for me, but don't be too carefree, the last time that happened it wasn't fair to me."
She said, "Hold me close and look into my eyes and please tell me you're finally my wonderful surprise?"

2-17-16

Afraid To Say

She was afraid to say, because of the little mistake she
made that day.
She knew when he found out, it wouldn't be okay.
One little slip, one little tip, it doesn't matter to him
because he will still trip.
She never said a word because she knew his hand would
slip.
She would try to hide and not let it slide and hope he
didn't find out what was on the inside. Because if he knew,
it would just start a fight.
She was scared and didn't have the strength to give up
her last might.

Inner Self

Find your inner self.
Don't try to be someone else.
For if you try to, you just might find what you have left
inside.
Don't try and hide, be proud and show your pride.
One day, you might fall off and never get back up to ride,
until you look at what you hide deep down inside.
You might find the strength to get back up and ride.
So keep holding on and stay strong, because one day you
will find just where you belong.

Miscellaneous

So Many Faces

So many faces and in so many places.
Some different, and so many races.
Each one different and a mind of their own.
Some are small and some are grown.
Brown skin, white skin, light skin, and dark.
Each individual with their own unique mark.
Small, tall, big, and fat, it's hard to imagine how different is
that.
Female and male, mix and match.
They each came out in their own little batch.
Or female and male, they were not all made well.
They each have their own story to tell.

Deep In The Battlefield

They fight deep in the battlefield,
For that's where they fight and train to kill.
The soldiers go out of their own will.
When one man dies, that's when they kneel.
It's hard to fight, and it's not a thrill.
When they hear the bombs, they know it's real.
For each warrior has their own appeal.
They all have stories they can't unveil.
Each one with their own side to tell.
Not every story ends well.
Some end up saying too-soon farewell.

They give up their lives to protect and fight.
They do their best and give all their might.
They give us our freedom and our right.
They're in the dark, but GOD gives them light.
He leads them on their journey and helps them feel
alright.
They fight till the end, for the battle we must win.
GOD goes out with them, to bring them safely in.

You Wear The Black and The Blue

You wear the black and the blue, but don't worry, we support you.
You may wear a gun, but relax, you can still have some fun.
You may be tired and may go home late, but you've worked hard and caught most of all the bad bait.
We appreciate you and all you do, and so glad to have officers just like you.
Our community is safe, thanks to you, we will always be here to back the people in blue.
We may not understand what you go through, but no matter what, we are here to back you.
This community would fall without the men/women dressed in blue.
That's why we are thankful for the officers like you.

In Memory of Two of Our Fallen Police Officers
In Honor Of Our Police Officers

My Bark Will Always Carry

My bark will always carry, and paw prints still around somewhere. Look around and you see them hidden there. I know my dog bed is empty, but for a while, you will still stare, but please don't worry, I'm in a better place now. Just know I'm always watching from up above, every now and then I will send you signs of my doggy love.

Just A Piece Of Paper

I'm just a piece of paper, until you fill me with words.
So pretty much free, like all the little birds.
So much blank space to fill, until you take me on an
adventurous thrill.
To tell a story that will give people a chill.
When you put the ink on my paper, it really gives me a
flavor.
When people start to read, they will see you did them a
favor.
So, fill me with adventure and a journey to travel, because
at the end of the page, the story will start to unravel.

Just A Piece Of Paper 2

I'm just a piece of paper, all blank and white.
So fill me in quickly with what is in sight.
Your mind must be wondering, because life is far from boring.
So tell us a story that is an adventure forming.
Maybe about a day when it was really storming.

Looking Out The Window

Looking out the window, wondering what's out there.
I see all the birds soaring high in the air.
The sky is baby blue, with a slight touch of white and grey
hue.
The sun shines bright and gives off all of its light.
The grass is bright green, and the animals and bugs know
what the signs mean.
Springtime has sprung, and it's time.

Home

Home is where my family roams.
Home is where we all belong.
It's hard to stay away too long.
Home is where we all get along.
The smell is so sweet, and it's just like a special treat.
You can't wait for the next time for your family to meet.
It's warm and cozy and so neat, leave the windows open to
hear the birds tweet.

About the Author

Ciara Lewis, born and raised in Kentucky, started writing poetry at the age of 12. She won her first poetry award in Middle School from an original poem she wrote for her grandma titled "Watching Over Me." This was just the beginning of her journey in poetry.

Ciara has a background in Medical Information Technology and Medical Billing/Coding. Ciara is the owner of KLConsulting LLC, a Medical Billing and Credentialing Business. Although her background is in Medical Billing, Ciara has always loved helping people through her poetry.

Ciara will not only produce poetry books but will, in the near future, put poetry on blankets, mugs, and more. She is going to be a guiding light for those who are interested in growing as a poet. Connect with Ciara via email at cecespoetrycorner@gmail.com

Website: http://fierceandfearlessentrepreneur.com
Facebook: https://www.facebook.com/fierceandfearlessentrepreneur/
Instagram: https://www.instagram.com/fierceandfearlessentrepreneur/